Contents

Macmillan Education
4 Crinan Street
London N1 9XW
A division of Macmillan Education Limited

Companies and representatives throughout the world

Mimi's Wheel Level 3 Pupil's Book ISBN 978-1-380-01876-2
Mimi's Wheel Level 3 Pupil's Book with Navio App ISBN 978-1-380-02715-3

First published 2019

Original design by Clare Webber
Page make-up by emc design ltd
Illustrated by Jose Ignacio Gómez (Nacho Gómez) pp3–52 (all character artwork and main illustrations); Conor Rawson (Beehive Illustration) pp11, 19, 20, 27, 28, 35, 36, 43, 44, 51 and 52 (Culture and Values illustrations); Animation Group Sp. z o.o. pp53–60, 70–72
Cover design by emc design ltd
Main cover illustration by Jose Ignacio Gómez (Nacho Gómez) with additional artwork by Conor Rawson (Beehive Illustration)
Picture research by Lorraine Beck

Author's acknowledgements
I would like to thank everyone at Macmillan Education in the UK, Spain and Mexico who has contributed to the development and production of these materials. I would also like to thank all the teachers who have taken time to read and pilot the materials, and given invaluable feedback at every stage of writing the course. Special thanks as ever go to my husband, Alan, for his encouragement and support, and to our son and daughter, Jamie and Hannah, from whose early childhood days I learnt so much.

The publishers would like to thank Alex Tamulis, São Paulo, Brazil; Ayşegül Sezer, İNO Schools, Turkey; Daniela Araujo Pielli, Alt Idiomas, São Bernardo Do Campo, Brazil; Daniela Pugliese, Milton's College, Buenos Aires, Argentina; Esra Ezici, Turkey; Fernanda Domeniconi Nery Amorim, São Paulo, Brazil; Gabriela Iocolari, English Schoolhouse, Buenos Aires, Argentina; Gulbin Cin, Bahcesehir College, Turkey; Mariana Pastorino, Em Pi Instituto de Inglés, Santa Fe, Argentina; Mariné Ortiz, Warrington, Buenos Aires, Argentina; Paola Daniela Tuninetti, Academia Argüello, Córdoba, Argentina; Silvana Paola Accardo, Escuela Cooperativa Mundo Nuevo Instituto Casa de Jesús, Buenos Aires, Argentina.

The authors and publishers would like to thank the following for permission to reproduce their photographs:
Alamy Stock Photo/Frankie Angel pp30, 64(dinner), Alamy Stock Photo/Stefan Ember pp29, 34, 64(brushing hair), Alamy Stock Photo/José Manuel Gelpi Díaz p61(thinking), Alamy Stock Photo/Victor Gladkiy p14, 62(trees), Alamy Stock Photo/Esa Hiltula pp13, 18, 62(roundabout), Alamy Stock Photo/Idea studio pp45, 46, 50, 66(pool), Alamy Stock Photo/IMAGEMORE Co. Ltd pp29, 34, 64(brushing teeth), Alamy Stock Photo/James Jackson pp30, 64(breakfast), Alamy Stock Photo/David Lee p38(tl), Alamy Stock Photo/Roel Meijer pp13, 18, 62(slide), Alamy Stock Photo/Monkey Business p25(parrots), Alamy Stock Photo/Robert Morris p33(house), Alamy Stock Photo/Pixavril p61(painting), Alamy Stock Photo/Apisit Sriputtirut pp21, 25, 26, 63(crocodile), Alamy Stock Photo/Anna Stowe pp45, 50, 66(toyshop), Alamy Stock Photo/Wavebreak Media Ltd pp46, 66(zoo), Alamy Stock Photo/John White Photos p49(m), Alamy Stock Photo/Zoonar GmbH pp38, 41, 65(spaghetti), **Getty Images** pp22, 63(monkey),Getty Images/AlexStar pp68,(modelling clay), Getty Images/Steve Allen p49(l), Getty Images/ allFOOD p65(rice), Getty Images/amriphoto pp21, 22, 25, 26, 63(elephant), Getty Images/artisteer pp30, 64(lunch), Getty Images/ bgfoto pp14, 62(grass), Getty Images/David Bishop Inc.pp37, 42, 65(chicken), Getty Images/ blue jean images RF/Lane Oatey p61, Getty Images/Carlsson, Peter pp46, 66(restaurant), Getty Images/ cenkertekin pp13, 18, 62(seesaw), Getty Images/ChiccoDodiFC p33(preschool), Getty Images/ cjmckendry pp13, 14, 18, 62(pond), Getty Images/ Clover No.7 Photography p61(running), Getty Images/DarioEgidi pp46, 66(supermarket), Getty Images/ Peter Dazeley pp30, 64(shower), Getty Images/Elva Etienne pp5, 10, 61(drawing), Getty Images/ EyeEm/Adzahar Saini pp13, 18, 62(swing), Getty Images/ fanjianhua pp14, 62(path), Getty Images/ Floortje pp37, 42, 65(pancake), 38(br), Getty Images/Stephen Frink p49(r), Getty Images/ GalapagosFrame pp14, 18(bench), Getty Images/GlobalP pp21, 26, 63(hippo, lion, parrot), p22, 63(hippo, parrot, snake, zebra), p25(monkeys), Getty Images/hallojulie pp17, 18(park), Getty Images/Hemera Technologies pp67,68 69, (paper), Getty Images/Hero Images pp45, 50, 66(museum), Getty Images/ImagesBazaar p13 (cl), 61(dancing), Getty Images/indigolotos p41(l), Getty Images/ iStockphoto pp22, 63(giraffe), 37, 38, 42, 65(yoghurt), Getty Images/iStockphoto/Thinkstock pp25(hippo), Getty Images/Juanmonino pp38, 65(sh), Getty Images/KidStock pp29, 34, 64(getting dressed), Getty Images/Dave King pp37, 38, 42, 65(toast), Getty Images/ kivoart p41(r), Getty Images/Philippe Lissac pp5, 10, 61(counting), Getty Images/ losw pp14, 17, 18bmr(roundabout), Getty Images/ luamduan pp22, 63(tiger), Getty Images/ lucielang pp67(tl),69(crayons), Getty Images/Rob Maynard pp46, 66(park), Getty Images/ MilaDrumeva p62(bench), Getty Images/ monkeybusinessimages pp29, 34, 64(washing hands), 45, 50(cinema), Getty Images/ Marvin E. Newman pp45, 46, 50, 66(shops), Getty Images/photohampster pp14, 62(flowers), Getty Images/ photka p14 (seesaw), Getty Images/pioneer111 pp14, 17, 18bmr(swings), Getty Images/RedHelga pp38, 65(pizza), Getty Images/Sergiy1975 p14(slide), Getty Images/somethingway pp5, 10, 61(singing), Getty Images/Spaces Images pp46, 66(bookshop), Getty Images/travellinglight pp38, 65(soup), Getty Images/Martin Wahlborg p14(park background), Getty Images/Wavebreakmedia pp29, 34, 64(getting up), Getty Images/Priscila Zambotto pp5, 10, 61(building), **Getty Images Plus**/iStock pp37, 42, 65(lettuce); **iStockphoto**/alex_kz pp67, 69, (glue); Springer Nature Limited/Paul Bricknell pp5, 10, 61(colouring), 64(washing face); **Shutterstock**/Serhii Bobyk p46, 66(cinema).

Commissioned photographs by Helen Marsden/Spectrecom pp4, 6, 7(Alex, Lucy), 9(Alex, Lucy, Auntie Vicky), 12, 10(bmr), 67(1, 2, 3), 14(Alex, Lucy), 15, 17(tr), 20, 22(Alex, Lucy), 23, 25(Alex, Lucy, Auntie Vicky), 28, 26(bmr), 68(1, 2, 3), 30(Alex, Lucy), 31, 33(tr), 34, 36, (bmr, br), 38(Alex, Lucy), 39, 41(Alex, Lucy, Auntie Vicky), 44(Alex, Lucy, Auntie Vicky), 42(br), 46(Alex, Lucy), 47, 49(tr), 50(br), 52, 69 (1, 2, 3).

Printed and bound in Spain

2025 2024 2023 2022 2021
16 15 14 13 12 11 10 9 8 7

Hello

How are you?

Listen and sing *Big Wheel*. Listen, point and say. Stick the number stickers. Circle your favourite number. Answer the questions. Language: Mummy, Daddy, Mimi, Dylan; Big Wheel; blue, green, orange, pink, red, yellow; numbers 1–6; Hello, how are you? I'm fine, thank you. Where's number (one)? It's on (red).

3

Watch. Listen to the story *Hurry up, Mummy!* Circle and colour the items Mimi and Dylan give Mummy. Answer the questions. Language: apple, hat, shoes, shorts, socks, t-shirt, water; late, sleepy; Hello. How are you? I'm (sleepy). Hurry up. Here's your (hat). Goodbye.

School
A new friend

Listen, point and repeat. Listen and stick the school activity stickers. Listen and play *Memory*. Circle the activities you like. Say. Language: colour, count, draw, paint, play, sing; blue, green, orange, pink, red, yellow; Where's (draw)? It's on (red).

1:21 hello 1:22 1:23

  1:24 1:25   hello

Listen and find the new school activities. Listen, point and sing *What do you do at school?* Match the activities to Lucy and Alex. Answer the question. Language: count, dance, draw, jump, paint, run, sing, think; What do you do at school? I (draw) at school.

6

1:27

Watch. Listen to the story _A new friend_. Circle who's new at school. Stick the story sticker.
Language: colour, count, dance, draw, jump, paint, run, sing, think; What do you do at school?
I (think) at school. Do you want to (colour)? Yes, I do. / No, I don't. I want to (jump).

  1:28

Watch. Listen, point and sing *Katy Kangaroo*. Trace ✔ or ✘ to show what Katy does and doesn't want to do. Trace and colour Katy. Answer the questions.
Language: colour, count, draw, jump, paint; Do you want to (draw)? No, I want to (jump).

8

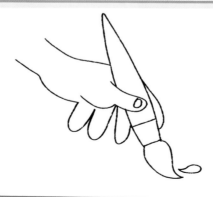

Watch. Listen and point. Circle what Alex and Lucy want to do. Colour what you want to do. Answer the questions. Language: colour, dance, draw, paint, play, sing; Do you want to (paint)? Yes. / No. I want to (sing).

9

I can...

Vocabulary

Story

Speaking

Circle the school activities you know. Listen, point and say. Listen and answer. Answer the questions. Complete the faces to show what you can do. Language: colour, count, dance, draw, jump, paint, play, run, sing, think; What do you do at school? I (draw) at school. Do you want to (sing)? Yes. / No. I want to (paint).

10

Listen and point to the story. Say. Colour the child being kind at school.

Language: colour, help, play, share, sit down; bag, banana, coat, crayons, friend, home, school; happy, sad; Do you want to (play)? I like/don't like (school). I'm (happy).

SOCIAL AND EMOTIONAL LEARNING

Culture

1 2 3 4

1

Watch. Listen, point and sing *Go in and out the window.* **Match and number the photos in order.**

Language: dance, go, shake hands, stand; partner, window; numbers 1–4

1:34

The park
Mimi's kite

?

1:35

hello

1:36

1:37

Listen, point and repeat. Listen and stick the park stickers. Listen and play *Memory*.
Circle the things in your park. Say. Language: bench, pond, roundabout, seesaw, slide,
swing; blue, green, orange, pink, red, yellow; Where's the (seesaw)? It's on (pink).

13

Listen and find the new park words. Listen, point and sing **There's a pond in the park.** Tick (✔) the park objects in the song. Say. **Language:** bench, flowers, grass, path, pond, roundabout, seesaw, slide, swings, trees; There's (a pond). There are (trees).

14

Lesson 3 — Story

Watch. Listen to the story *Mimi's kite*. Circle the weather in the story. Stick the story sticker.
Language: bench, flowers, kite, path, pond, slide, swings, trees, windy; It's (windy). There's the (pond). There are the (flowers). Is there (a slide)? Are there (swings)? Where's (Mummy)? Under the (tree). On the (bench).

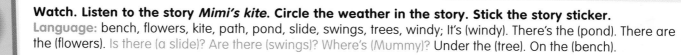

Lesson 4 — Story Song

The park

1 2 3 4 5

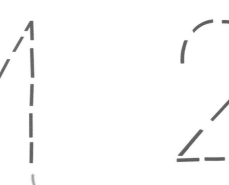   

1:42

Watch. Listen, point and sing *Fly the kite*. **Trace the numbers. Match the numbers and pictures in order. Say.** Language: flowers, kite, pond, trees; numbers 1–4; There's the (pond). There are the (trees).

Speaking

Life skills

The park

1:44

hello

Watch. Listen and point. Circle what's in the park. Answer the questions. Language:
bench, flowers, grass, path, pond, roundabout, seesaw, slide, swings, trees; Is there (grass)?
Are there (trees)? There's (a roundabout). There are (swings).

17

I can...

Vocabulary

Story

Speaking

Circle the park words you know. Listen, point and say. Listen and answer. Answer the question. Complete the faces to show what you can do. Language: bench, flowers, grass, path, pond, roundabout, seesaw, slide, swing, trees; What's in the park? There's (a pond). There are (flowers).

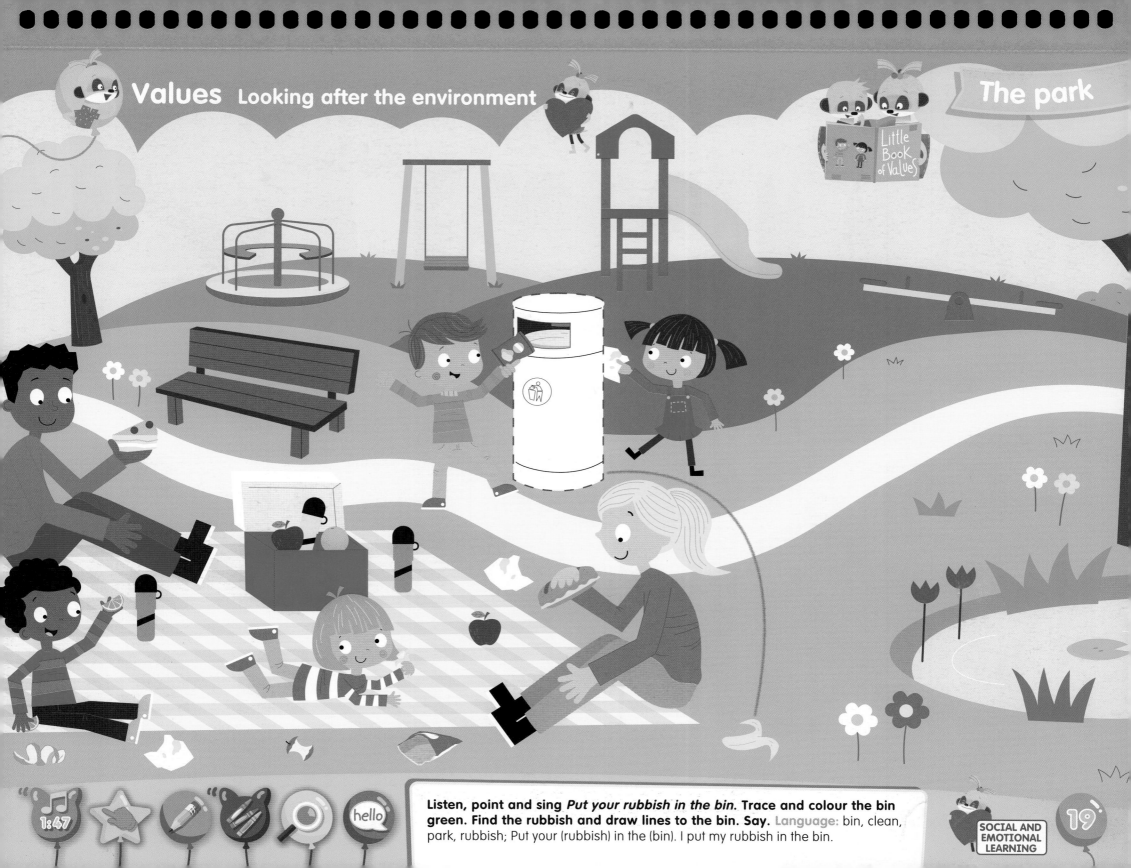

Listen, point and sing *Put your rubbish in the bin*. **Trace and colour the bin green. Find the rubbish and draw lines to the bin. Say.** Language: bin, clean, park, rubbish; Put your (rubbish) in the (bin). I put my rubbish in the bin.

SOCIAL AND EMOTIONAL LEARNING

19

 **Culture**

Watch. Listen and point to the story *Little Red Riding Hood*. **Circle the words you hear in the story. Say.** Language: apples, biscuits, cake, ears, eyes, flowers, house, path, teeth, trees, wolf; There are (trees).

20

Wild animals
The surprise

Listen, point and repeat. Listen and stick the wild animal stickers. Listen and play
***Memory*. Circle the animals you like. Say.** Language: crocodile, elephant, hippo, lion,
monkey, parrot; blue, green, orange, pink, red, yellow; Where's the (crocodile)? It's on (green).

 ✔

 2:04   2:05   hello

Listen and find the new wild animals. Listen, point and sing *What's that?* Tick (✔) the animals Alex and Lucy see. Answer the question. Language: elephant, giraffe, hippo, monkey, parrot, snake, tiger, zebra; colours; What's that? It's (a snake). It's (black and white). It's got (big teeth).

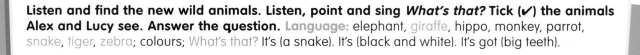

Watch. Listen to the story *The surprise*. **Circle Mimi's birthday present to Dylan. Stick the story sticker. Language:** binoculars; crocodile, lion, monkey, parrot, snake, tiger; colours; What's that? It's a (tiger). It's got (big eyes). I'm a (crocodile).

2:08

hello

Watch. Listen, point and sing *The party surprise*. **Match the animals and characters. Circle your favourite animal and character. Answer the question.** Language: crocodile, lion, monkey, parrot, snake, tiger; What's that? It's a (snake). I'm a (tiger).

Life skills

  2:10   hello

Watch. Listen and point. Tick (✔) the wild animals Auntie Vicky, Alex and Lucy see at the safari park. Draw a wild animal you want to see. Answer the question. Language: crocodile, elephant, hippo, monkey, parrot; What's that? It's (an elephant). It's got (big ears).

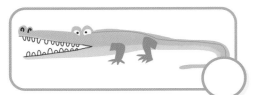

I can ...

Vocabulary

Story

Speaking

  2:11 hello 2:12

Colour the circles of the wild animals you know. Listen, point and say. Listen and answer. Answer the question. Complete the faces to show what you can do. Language: crocodile, elephant, giraffe, hippo, lion, monkey, parrot, snake, tiger, zebra; What's that? It's (an elephant). It's (grey). It's got (big ears).

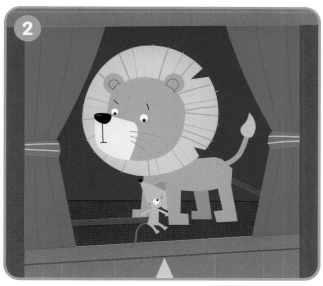

Listen and point to the story. Say. Colour the children saying 'thank you'.
Language: lion, mouse; head, teeth; I'm hungry. I can help you! Thank you.

SOCIAL AND EMOTIONAL LEARNING

Wild animals

Watch. Listen, point and sing *Five little monkeys*. **Trace the numbers. Trace and colour the monkeys. Say.** Language: crocodile, monkey; numbers 1–5; (Five) little monkeys sitting in a tree. You can't catch me! Along comes Mr Crocodile.

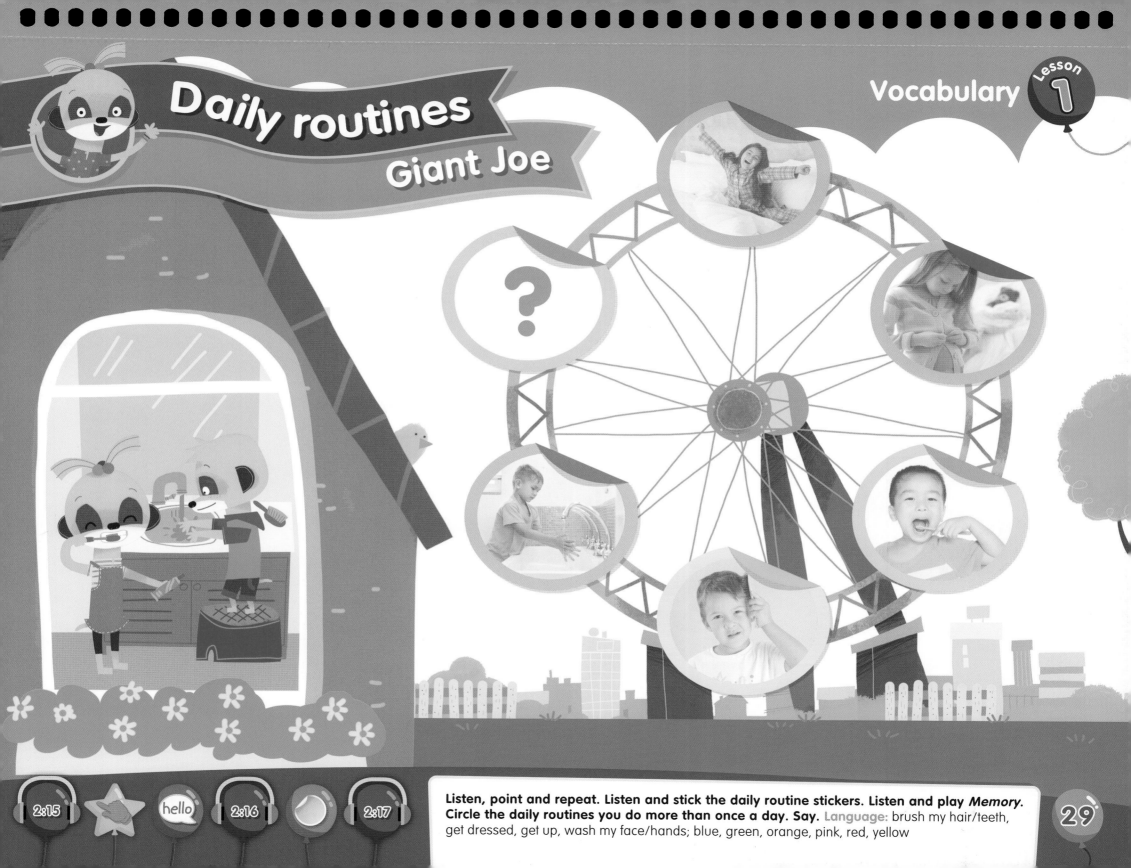

?

Listen, point and repeat. Listen and stick the daily routine stickers. Listen and play *Memory*.
Circle the daily routines you do more than once a day. **Say. Language:** brush my hair/teeth,
get dressed, get up, wash my face/hands; blue, green, orange, pink, red, yellow

2:15   hello   2:16   2:17

29

2:18   2:19   hello

Listen and find the new daily routines. Listen, point and sing *What do you do every day?* Tick (✔)
the routines in the song. Draw a routine. Say. Language: brush my hair/teeth, get dressed, get up,
have a shower, have breakfast/lunch/dinner, wash my face/hands; I (have lunch).

30

Watch. Listen to the story *Giant Joe*. Circle what Grandpa's story is about. Stick the story sticker. Language: brush my hair/teeth, get dressed, get up, have breakfast/dinner, wash my face/hands; Do you (wash your hands)? Yes, I do. I (get up). It's time to (get dressed).

31

Story Song

2:22

hello

Watch. Listen, point and sing *Giant Joe's day*. Circle the routines Giant Joe does every day. Answer the questions. Language: brush my hair/teeth, get dressed, get up, have a shower, have breakfast/lunch/dinner, wash my face/hands; Do you (wash your face)? Yes. / No. I (brush my hair).

32

Daily routines

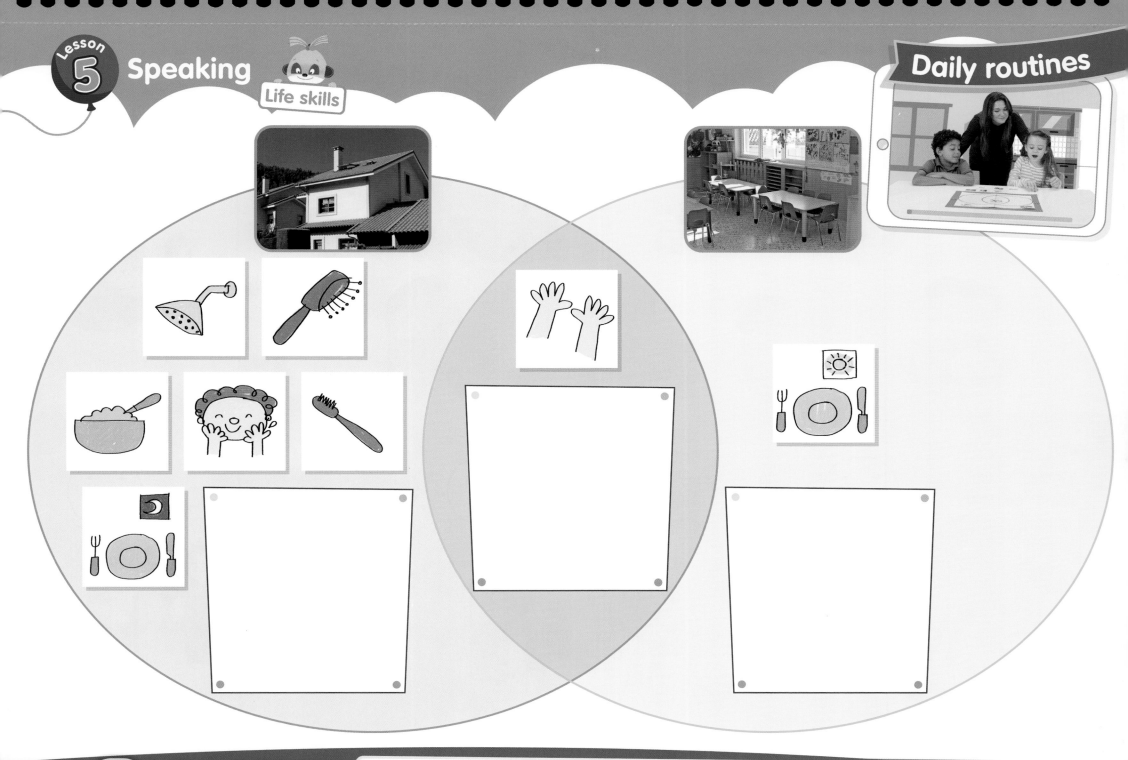

  2:24   hello

Watch. Listen and point. Draw three of your routines in the diagram. Answer the questions.
Language: brush my hair/teeth, have a shower, have breakfast/lunch/dinner, wash my face/hands; home, school; What do you do at (home)? I (have breakfast) at (home). Do you (have lunch) at (school)? Yes. / No.

33

Daily routines

I can...

Vocabulary	Story	Speaking

  2:25   hello 2:26

Circle the routines you know. Listen, point and say. Listen and answer. Answer the questions. Complete the faces to show what you can do. Language: brush my hair/teeth, get dressed, get up, have a shower, have breakfast/lunch/dinner, wash my face/hands; What do you do every day? I (get up). Do you (have lunch) at (home)? Yes. / No.

Listen, point and sing *I sleep, I eat, I learn, I play.* **Tick (✔) the daily routines you do. Say.** Language: brush my teeth, drink water, eat, have a shower, learn, play, sleep, wash my hands; I (drink water) every day.

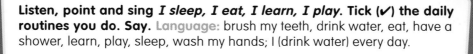

SOCIAL AND EMOTIONAL LEARNING

35

 **Culture**

1

2

3

4

  2:28   hello

Watch. Listen and point to the story *Goldilocks and the three bears*. **Draw and colour a picture to show what you think happens next. Say.** Language: bed, bowl, chair; big, small, tiny; Mummy, Daddy, Baby Bear; This (bowl) is (small).

Meals
Toast, toast, toast!

Listen, point and repeat. Listen and stick the food stickers. Listen and play *Memory*. Circle the food you like. Say. Language: chicken, pancake, rice, salad, toast, yogurt; blue, green, orange, pink, red, yellow

 3:04   3:05   hello

Listen and find the new food words. Listen, point and sing *What do you have for breakfast?* Match the food to Alex and Lucy. Answer the questions. Language: chicken, fish, pancakes, pizza, rice, salad, soup, spaghetti, toast, yogurt; breakfast, lunch, dinner; What do you have for (dinner)? I have (soup).

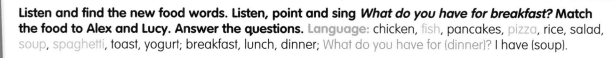

38

Watch. Listen to the story *Toast, toast, toast!* Circle the food Mimi wants for every meal. Stick the story sticker.
Language: chicken, fish, pancakes, peas, pizza, rice, salad, soup, spaghetti, toast, yogurt; breakfast, lunch, dinner;
What do you have for (breakfast)? I have (yogurt). Do you want (pancakes)? I want (toast), please.

39

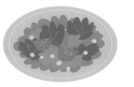

 3:08

 hello

Watch. Listen, point and sing *The toast song*. **Circle** 😊 **or** ☹️ **to show the food Mimi wants and doesn't want. Answer the questions. Language:** chicken, pancakes, pizza, rice, salad, soup, spaghetti, toast, yogurt; Do you want (chicken)? Yes, please. / No, thank you. I want/don't want (toast).

40

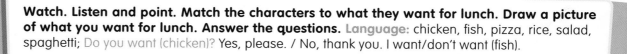

Watch. Listen and point. Match the characters to what they want for lunch. Draw a picture of what you want for lunch. Answer the questions. Language: chicken, fish, pizza, rice, salad, spaghetti; Do you want (chicken)? Yes, please. / No, thank you. I want/don't want (fish).

Lesson 6 Review

  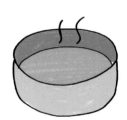  

I can ...

Vocabulary

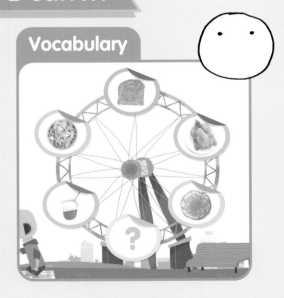

Story

Speaking

  3:11   hello 3:12

Circle the food you know. Listen, point and say. Listen and answer. Answer the questions. Complete the faces to show what you can do. Language: chicken, fish, pancake, pizza, rice, salad, soup, spaghetti, toast, yogurt; breakfast, lunch, dinner; What do you have for (lunch)? I have (rice). Do you want (soup)? Yes. / No.

Listen and point to the story. Draw a picture of food you want to try. Answer the questions.
Language: carrots, food, peas, soup, tomatoes; green, orange, red; Do you want (peas)?
Yes, please. / No, thank you. I like/don't like (soup).

SOCIAL AND EMOTIONAL LEARNING

1   2   3   4   5

Watch. Listen, point and sing _Mix a pancake_. Match and number the pictures in order. Say. Language: pan, pancake; catch, cook, mix, toss; numbers 1–5; (Mix) the pancake.

Town
A day out

?

Listen, point and repeat. Listen and stick the town stickers. Listen and play *Memory*.
Circle the places you go to. Say. Language: cinema, museum, shopping centre,
swimming pool, toy shop, zoo; blue, green, orange, pink, red, yellow

3:15 hello 3:16 3:17

Listen and find the new town words. Listen, point and sing *Do you want to go to the zoo?* Tick (✔) where Alex and Lucy want to go. Answer the questions. Language: bookshop, cinema, park, restaurant, shopping centre, supermarket, swimming pool, zoo; Do you want to go to the (zoo)?

Lesson 3 Story

DINOSAURS IN SPACE

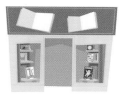

3:21

Watch. Listen to the story *A day out*. Circle the places Mimi and Dylan go to. Stick the story sticker.

Language: bookshop, cinema, museum, shopping centre, toy shop; dinosaurs, space; Do you want to go to the (cinema)? Yes, I do. / No, I don't. I want to go to the (museum). Let's go to the (shopping centre).

47

DINOSAURS IN SPACE

3:22

hello

Watch. Listen, point and sing *Dinosaurs in space*. **Match Mimi and Dylan to what they want to do. Point and say. Draw a picture of something you want to learn about.** Language: cinema; books, dinosaurs, space, toys; go, learn, play, read; I want to play with (dinosaur) toys. I want to learn about (animals).

Life skills

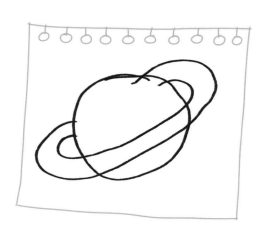

  3:24   hello

Watch. Listen and point to the photos. Match Alex and Lucy's pictures to the parts of the museum. Colour the things you want to see. Answer the questions. Language: dinosaurs, fish, planet, sea, space; museum; Do you want to (see the fish)? Yes, please. / No, thank you. I want to (learn about dinosaurs).

Town

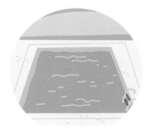

I can ...

Vocabulary

Story

DiNOSAURS iN SPACE

Speaking

  3:25   hello 3:26

Circle the town words you know. Listen, point and say. Listen and answer. Answer the questions. Complete the faces to show what you can do. Language: bookshop, cinema, museum, park, restaurant, shopping centre, supermarket, swimming pool, toy shop, zoo; Do you want to go to the (zoo)? Yes. / No. I want to go to the (park).

Values Interest in learning

3:27

hello

Listen, point and sing *I find out about my world*. Tick (✔) the ways you learn. Draw a picture to show a way you like to learn. Say. Language: ask questions, find out about my world, go to school, look at books, play games, talk to friends, watch films/TV; I want to learn. Do you?

SOCIAL AND EMOTIONAL LEARNING

Culture

     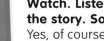

Watch. Listen and point to the story *The enormous carrot*. **Colour the things in the story. Say.** Language: carrot; boy, girl, man, woman; pull; Do you want to help? Yes, of course. The (man) pulls the (woman).

Colours

Listen, point and say. Colour the animals the same as in the pictures.
Colour the circle of your favourite animal. Say.
Language: black, blue, red, white, yellow; It's (red).

Colours

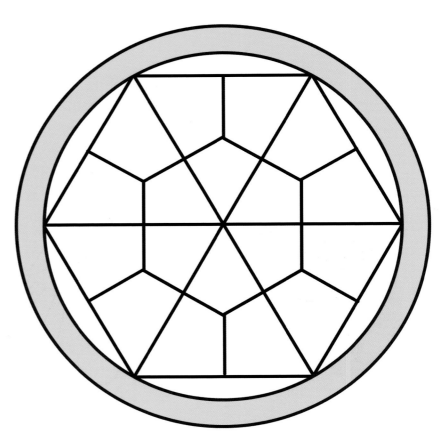

Listen, point and say. Complete the pattern. Create your own colour pattern. Say.
Language: brown, green, orange, pink, purple; It's (orange).

54

Listen, point and say. Trace the numbers. Draw lines to join the numbers in order. Circle your favourite number. Say.
Language: numbers 1–10; It's (six).

Numbers 123

1 2 3 4 5 6 7 8 9 10

Listen, point and say. Count the animals and write the numbers. Say.
Language: numbers 1–10; There are (three) (dogs). There's one (mouse).

Shapes

Listen, point and say. Draw and colour the next shape in the sequence. Say.
Language: circle, diamond, star; It's a (star).

Shapes

hello

Listen, point and say. Use triangles, squares and rectangles to draw a picture. Say.
Language: rectangle, square, triangle; It's a (triangle).

Concepts

Listen, point and say. Circle the pictures of hungry children red.
Circle the pictures of thirsty children blue. Say.
Language: hungry, thirsty; I'm (hungry).

Concepts

Listen, point and say. Find and circle six differences in the pictures that show clean and dirty. Say.

Language: clean, dirty; It's (clean).

60

School

| colour | count | dance | draw | jump |

| paint | play | run | sing | think |

Picture Dictionary

bench

flowers

grass

path

pond

roundabout

seesaw

slide

swing

trees

Picture Dictionary

crocodile

elephant

giraffe

hippo

lion

monkey

parrot

snake

tiger

zebra

Picture Dictionary

brush my hair

brush my teeth

get dressed

get up

have a shower

have breakfast

have dinner

have lunch

wash my face

wash my hands

Picture Dictionary

chicken	fish	pancake	pizza	rice

salad	soup	spaghetti	toast	yogurt

bookshop

cinema

museum

park

restaurant

shopping centre

supermarket

swimming pool

toy shop

zoo

Project 1

COOPERATIVE LEARNING

1

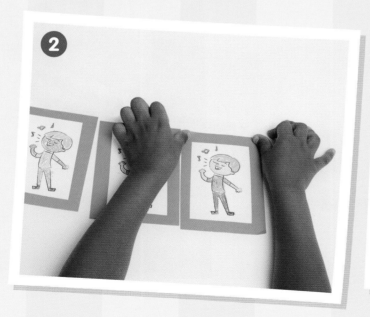

2

3

Our favourite school activities

Choose and colour your favourite school activity. Stick your picture on the chart. Answer the questions. Language: dance, paint, play, sing; colours; numbers; chart, fantastic, great, picture; What do you do at school? I (dance) at school. How many people (dance)? (Four). Do you want to (paint)? Yes. / No. I want to (play). Our chart is (fantastic).

Project 2

COOPERATIVE LEARNING

1

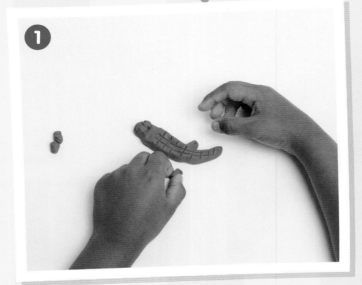

2

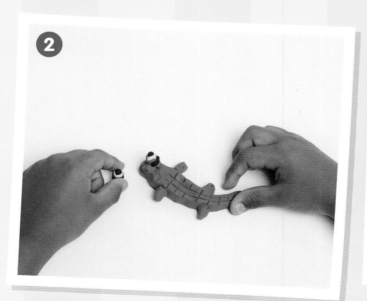

3

Our safari park

Make a wild animal. Put your animals together to make a safari park. Answer the questions. Language: crocodile, elephant, giraffe, hippo, lion, monkey, parrot, snake, tiger, zebra; colours; What's that? It's (a zebra). It's (black and white). It's got (a tail). I like the (giraffe). Do you like the (crocodile)? Yes. / No.

Project 3

COOPERATIVE LEARNING

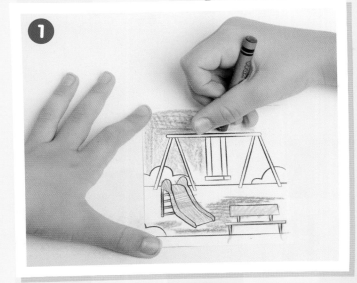
1

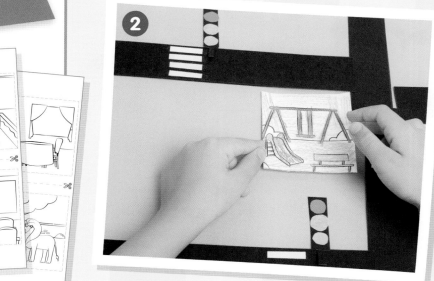
2

3

Mimi's town

hello

Choose and colour a place. Put the places together to make a map of Mimi's town. Answer the questions.
Language: bookshop, cinema, park, restaurant, supermarket, swimming pool, toy shop, zoo; colours; Do you want to go to the (restaurant)? Do you like the (zoo)? Yes. / No. I want to go to the (supermarket). I like the (park). The (cinema) is (blue).

69

3:36

hello

3:37

Listen, point and say. Listen and sing *We love books*. **Match the books. Choose and colour the cover of the book you like best. Say.** Language: animals, people, pictures, stories, words, world; I like books about (people). I like books with (pictures).

Festivals

World Animal Day

3:38    **3:39**

Listen, point and say. Listen and sing *Save the rhino*. Find and circle the animals in the song. Draw and colour an animal you want to save. Say.
Language: elephant, gorilla, panda, polar bear, rhino, tiger; Save the (panda).

1
2
3
4

1

3:40 hello 3:41

Listen, point and say. Listen and sing *When we go to the countryside*. Number the pictures in the order of the song. Draw a picture of you in the places you go to. Say.

Language: countryside, mountains, seaside, woods; I go to the (countryside).

72

Hello

School

The park

Wild animals

Daily routines

Meals

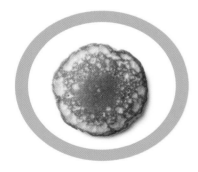

Town